# MASTERING
# SUSHI

ÉDITIONS TOTAL
PUBLISHING
QUEBECOR MEDIA

RESEARCH AND TEXT : Gino Lepore, Kathe Lieber,
REVISERS : Momoe Amano, Judith Berman, Emiko Kosuge
SUSHI CHEF : Shinji Nagai
PHOTOGRAPHER : Annie Pomminville/Groupimage
FOOD STYLIST : Marina Alberti
GRAPHIC DESIGN : RoweDesign
PUBLICATION DIRECTOR : Gino Lepore

Total Publishing acknowledges the financial support of the
Government of Canada through the Book Publishing Industry
Development program for its publishing activities; The SODEC and
Government of Québec - Tax credit for book publishing -
Administered by SODEC.

ISBN 2-89535-006-X

Legal deposit, 2003
Bibliothèque nationale du Québec

Printed in China

ÉDITIONS TOTAL PUBLISHING
7, chemin Bates
Outremont (Qc) Canada
H2V 4V7

National Library of Canada cataloguing in publication
Lepore, Gino
Mastering sushi : understanding the menu
Includes index.
ISBN 2-89535-006-X
1. Sushi. 2. Cookery, Japanese. I. Lieber, Kathe. II. Title.
TX724.5.J3L46 2003   641.5952   C2003-940905-8

# ■THE SUSHI EXPERIENCE

Sushi is the ideal food to share with family and friends. It's a glorious treat for the eyes and the taste buds, and it's so much fun to eat!

Sushi is also one of those "perfect" foods. Low in fat, cholesterol and calories, and high in protein, carbohydrates, minerals and vitamins, it is balanced, nutritious and easy on the stomach.

What's more, the ritual and sense of ceremony associated with sushi provide a welcome opportunity to escape from our hectic world for a while.

*Bon appétit!*

*Special thanks to Tri-Du, Lan Tran, Tommy Provias,*
*Colette Laberge and Marc Laberge.*

# ∎TABLE OF CONTENTS

**4** THE ART OF SUSHI
The origins of sushi; nutritional and other information about this healthy food; accom paniments; how to eat sushi and sashimi; plus other interesting details about the *art of sushi.*

**18** ON THE MENU
A selection of sushi, complete with ingredients and tantalizing photographs. A clear, basic explanation of what's in the sushi you are about to eat, plus suggestions fo continuing your explorations of the world of sushi. Japanese Etiquette, Culinary Tips, plus useful expressions round out the section. Also included, a rating scale you can note how you like this particular sushi.

**72** THE ESSENTIALS
From abura age to yukiwa-maki, a glossary of the key words organized alphabetically.

**92** MY FAVOURITE
SUSHI BARS AND RESTAURANTS
Write down the names of your favourite sushi-bars and restaurants.

**94** INDEX "ON THE MENU"

# ■THE ART OF SUSHI

## A QUICK HISTORY OF SUSHI

It makes perfect sense that sushi was "invented" in Japan,
an island nation surrounded by seas that teem with a huge
array of fish and shellfish. The other key ingredient, rice, is
grown on terraced plots in the mountainous parts of the country.
In such a densely populated nation, the twin blessings of
sea and soil have always been greatly valued.

Around the seventh century C.E., the Japanese developed
a method for preserving fish by pressing cleaned, raw fish
between layers of salt and rice, with a stone on top. After a
few weeks, the stone would be replaced with a light cover,
and the fish would be left to ferment for a few months
until it was ready to eat. Originally, the rice was discarded,
until some unknown thrifty cook realized what a waste
that was.

Fermentation finally went by the wayside in 1824, when
a clever chef called Hanaya Yohei had the bright idea of
serving the fish in a form that closely resembles today's
sushi – an event that inspired a famous poem. Two
distinct styles soon emerged. Kansai style, which took its
name from Osaka in the Kansai region, featured sushi
mainly made of seasoned rice, combined with other
ingredients in beautifully presented edible packages. Edo
style (Tokyo was called Edo until 1868) was nigiri-zushi, with
a morsel of seafood sitting on a small pad of seasoned rice.

While the more ornamental Kansai style is still popular in Japan, Edo-style nigiri-zushi is more closely associated with the artistry of the sushi tradition. Until well into the twentieth century, street vendors would sell sushi, kept on a bed of ice covered with a bamboo mat, to businessmen or bathers leaving the public bathhouse. Since 1961, National Sushi Day has been celebrated in Japan every November 1 with an elaborate competition among sushi chefs.

In Japanese cooking, the virtuosity of the chef is second only to the quality and beauty of the ingredients. A great many Japanese dishes are served uncooked or lightly cooked, in small, elegant portions. Presentation is everything.

**THE SNAKE**
AVOCADO, SHRIMP TEMPURA, TOBIKO, MAYONNAISE, CUCUMBER, RICE, MASAGO, NORI

# ■THE ART OF SUSHI

### THE SUSHI BAR

The highly developed Japanese sense of aesthetics is reflected not only in the way food is served, but in the setting as well. While North Americans enjoy entertaining at home, most Japanese live in small houses and use the sushi bar or restaurant as a surrogate living room. Business and social meetings alike take place in restaurants, and the Japanese expect a high level of hospitality and sophistication when they go out. Many a friendship has been cemented and many a business deal anointed with sake in the intimate setting of the sushi bar.

Behind the counter of the sushi bar, the spotlight is on the chef, who wields his knife in front of the diners, making sushi to order and presenting it with great panache. Impeccable service, the freshest food, and elegant presentation are expected and valued.

## FRESHNESS IS THE KEY

The head chef selects the day's fish himself and demands the very best from his suppliers. He looks for shiny skin, firm fragrant flesh, bright red gills, and clear eyes. The fish should smell like the ocean, not "fishy."

Sashimi should be prepared from fish taken fresh from the clearest waters, iced but not frozen. Freshwater fish are rarely if ever served as sashimi due to the possibility of parasites. Salmon is always served marinated or smoked.

Many fish, such as tuna, freeze well, but some loss of flavour and succulence is inevitable during the thawing process. In the hands of a savvy sushi chef, properly frozen and thawed fish can taste nearly as good as fresh.

## A WORD OF WARNING

Pregnant women, very young children, the elderly, and those with vulnerable immune systems should be cautious about eating sashimi. The best way to make sure you will not encounter parasites is to patronize an establishment where the chef has uncompromising standards, but you might want to switch to vegetarian sushi. You will still find a great variety to choose from.

# ■THE ART OF SUSHI

## TYPES OF SUSHI
Sushi comes in many forms, the most common types being nigiri-zushi (handmade sushi), and maki-zushi (rolled sushi made with a bamboo mat).

## NIGIRI-ZUSHI
(Also spelled nigiri.) Meaning "pressed by hand," nigiri-zushi is a slice of cooked or uncooked fish lying across a pad of rice. The ingredients are then gently pressed together.

Known as "boat-style" sushi, gunkan is a type of nigiri-zushi where the fish and rice are held together with a band of seaweed, the whole resembling a little boat. This method is often used for smaller ingredients like fish roe.

Nigiri-zushi is often served with wasabi and dipped in soy sauce.

## MAKI-ZUSHI
(Also spelled maki.) Rolled sushi, made by wrapping rice, fish, and other ingredients into a long seaweed roll, which is then cut into bite-sized slices.

There are three types of maki-zushi rolls: futomaki, hosomaki, a slender roll cut into six small pieces, and temaki, literally, hand roll sushi, which resembles a small ice cream cone and is eaten in two or three bites.

Maki-zushi is served with soy sauce and gari.

Maki-zushi is said to have originated in eighteenth-century gambling houses in Japan, where gamers wanted something easy to eat while gambling.

## IT'S NOT ALL RAW

Contrary to popular belief, not all sushi is raw. Tempura maki-zushi, for instance, is a kind of temaki with lightly battered, deep-fried vegetables served in a nori cone. Many types of sushi also use smoked or marinated fish. All of these basic fish-cutting methods require an extremely sharp, heavy knife.

SHRIMP AND
EGGPLANT
TEMPURA

## VEGETARIAN SUSHI

California rolls (made without crab meat) are the most popular form of vegetarian sushi, but that's just the tip of the iceberg. Vegetarians who eat fish, of course, can enjoy the full range of sushi varieties; those who do not still have quite a range to choose from, with vegetables used creatively and presented beautifully in original ways.

# ■THE ART OF SUSHI

## USING THE CONDIMENTS

### SHOYU

The flavourful dark soy sauce known as shoyu is essential to
the sushi experience. The small shallow dish is for shoyu:
pour some from the bottle on the table and dip your sushi
into it. Pour as much as you think you will need, keeping
in mind that you can always add more. It is considered
poor form to fill the dish to the brim like a wading pool.

Don't drown your sushi. Shoyu is intended to complement,
not overwhelm, the flavour of sushi, and the purpose is to
flavour the fish, not the rice. Dip the top of the sushi (rice
side up) lightly into the soy sauce; do not soak the whole
piece. Then place the sushi in your mouth so that the fish
hits your taste buds.

### WASABI

The green paste traditionally served with sushi is a
Japanese horseradish called wasabi.

Although many people mix a little
wasabi into the shoyu with their
chopstick, this is not an authentic
practice. Instead, use your
chopstick to place a little
bit of wasabi directly on
the piece of sushi.

(While wasabi is served with nigiri zushi, it's not meant to be used.) The main thing to remember about wasabi is that it's very strong. So be careful and use only a tiny, tiny dab: you don't want to overwhelm the taste of the fish or the topping. Really intense wasabi is sometimes called namida, which means tears. If you've ever consumed more wasabi than you meant to and felt as though your head was about to explode, you'll understand the term!

## GARI

That little mound of thinly sliced pink vegetable is pickled ginger, called gari. Gari and wasabi are the condiments traditionally eaten with sushi. Gari is essential for refreshing your palate between bites of different types of sushi. Think of it as a palate cleanser, like the sorbet served between courses at gourmet restaurants. It's not considered good form to pile your sushi high with gari.

# ∎THE ART OF SUSHI

## NUTRITIONAL INFORMATION

If you need to justify your sushi addiction, it's easy to do on nutritional grounds. For those who are watching their weight, note that the leaner fish contain fewer than 100 calories per 100 grams, while the fattier varieties, such as mackerel, eel, and tuna, still come in at under 200. Cooked rice contains about 100 calories per 100 grams. (Watch the sake, however, at 239 calories a cup!)

### FISH
Fish is high in protein, low in fat, and very easy to digest. And here's the ultimate justification: the Japanese consider seafood to be an aphrodisiac. Whether that is true or not, the camaraderie and sensual pleasures of a sushi meal may well lead to romance.

### RICE
Rice is an excellent source of complex carbohydrates and dietary fibre. The fibre makes you feel full and helps digest your food, while the carbohydrates provide energy that is released slowly, producing a feeling of fullness.

### OILY FISH
All seafood is low in calories. The small amount of fat that fish contains is the "right" kind of fat, rich in Omega-3 fatty acids, so it's heart-healthy. (Omega-3 fatty acids can reduce the risk of heart attack by preventing the formation of blood clots that block arteries.)

## GARI

The healthy properties of ginger are well known.
It facilitates digestion and can help the body fend off
colds and the flu virus.

## WASABI

Wasabi is an excellent source of Vitamin C.

## SOY

Soybeans, used to make tofu, soy sauce, and miso,
provide high-quality protein. They also contain starch,
dietary fibre, some B-group vitamins, and various minerals –
as well as fat in the form of polyunsaturated oil. Soy is
also beneficial to women going through menopause, as
it contains phytoestrogens, the plant form of estrogen.

## NORI

Seaweed is an excellent source of iodine, calcium, and iron
– all needed to maintain healthy blood and bone structure.
It is also high in Vitamin B12, which is normally only found
in animal products – a plus for vegetarian sushi lovers.

# ■ THE ART OF SUSHI

## HOW TO EAT SUSHI AND SASHIMI : CHOPSTICKS OR FINGERS?

Use hashi (chopsticks) if you can manipulate them confidently (practice makes perfect). There's nothing wrong with using your fingers, however. Chopsticks are de rigueur for sashimi and maki sushi, but nigiri sushi (hand-rolled sushi) is considered finger food.

One bite or two? That depends on the size of the sushi, which tends to be bigger in North America.

Knives and forks are rarely seen at sushi bars. In fact, using western-style cutlery would be at best gauche and at worst insulting to the chef.

Many sushi lovers enjoy grazing from others' plates. This is fine, but when you pick up a delectable morsel from a friend's plate, make sure you turn your chopsticks around and use the other end.

## WHAT TO EXPECT WHEN YOU EAT
## IN A SUSHI BAR.

In North America, your meal will probably begin with miso soup, a flavourful broth with small cubes of tofu in it. After that, you will be offered an assortment of sashimi (just fish, no rice) and then comes the sushi. People usually eat the maki-zushi and the temaki first, because the crisp nori goes soft if it sits for very long. Before switching to the nigiri- zushi, it's a good idea to change the soy sauce for dipping. Dessert is served at the end of the meal.

More advanced sushi eaters, when ordering nigiri, might want to start with light-tasting white fish such as suzuki, ika or hotate, moving on to richer-tasting sushi such as maguro and hamachi and then finishing with toro and uni. This way, you can fully enjoy the delicate taste of white fish at the start and appreciate the richness of the more savoury fish later.

MISO SOUP

# ■THE ART OF SUSHI

## WHAT TO DRINK WITH SUSHI

Rule number one: no hard liquor, which anaesthetizes the taste buds. The following are the beverages that go best with sushi.

## TEA
Japanese tea is served throughout the meal. Green tea brings out the flavour of sushi, removes any aftertastes, and freshens the mouth for the next serving.

## BEER
Most Japanese restaurants in North America offer both Japanese beer (popular brands include Sapporo, Kirin, and Asahi) and local brews.

## WINE

While many sushi experts feel that wine overpowers
the delicate flavours of the fish and rice, there are some
"neutral" wines that make good companions for sushi. Try
a Pinot noir, Sancerre, or Sauvignon blanc. Champagne or
Riesling would also go down easily.

## SAKE

Sake is Japanese rice wine, made
from fermented rice. It is served
warm, before you eat – not during or
after. There is a ritual involved in
the drinking of sake, starting with
pouring the first drink for
someone else.

# AJI
# MACKEREL

Spanish Mackerel
Rice
Wasabi

Ginger
(Green onion)

## IF YOU LIKE AJI, TRY
IWASHI, SABA, *SAYORI*

## A LESSON IN JAPANESE
*Arigato.*
Thank you. (informal)

HOW I RATE
THIS SUSHI

## ALASKA

| Smoked salmon | Lettuce | Mayonnaise |
| Crab | Cucumber | Wasabi |
| Smelt fish roe | Rice | Nori |

**IF YOU LIKE ALASKA, TRY**
CALIFORNIA ROLL, MASAGO

**SUSHI ETIQUETTE**
The green tea is always taken clear, without
milk or sugar, and piping hot. It is perfectly
acceptable to slurp your tea.

**HOW I RATE THIS SUSHI**

# AMA-EBI

## SWEET SHRIMP

Sweet shrimp
Rice
Wasabi

**IF YOU LIKE AMA-EBI, TRY**
*BOTAN-EBI*, EBI, TEMPURA SHRIMP (see page 9)

**A LESSON IN JAPANESE**
*Oaiso.*
The bill or check.

**HOW I RATE THIS SUSHI**

# ANAGO
# SEA EEL

Sea eel
Rice

## IF YOU LIKE ANAGO, TRY
SALMON SKIN, UNAGI

## CULINARY TIP
Sea eel is always boiled first, then grilled. Because it is served with a special mixture of sugar, soy sauce, and eel stock, no dipping sauce or wasabi is needed.

HOW I RATE
THIS SUSHI

# AVOCADO
## AVOCADO

| | |
|---|---|
| Avocado | Nori |
| Rice | Sesame seeds |
| Wasabi (or mayonnaise) | |

## IF YOU LIKE AVOCADO, TRY
KAPPA MAKI, OSHINKO MAKI

## A LESSON IN JAPANESE
*Dozo*.
Please.

HOW I RATE
THIS SUSHI

# BENI JAKE

## PACIFIC SALMON

Pacific salmon
Rice
Wasabi

**IF YOU LIKE BENI JAKE, TRY**
KUNSEI SYAKE, MAGURO, SYAKE

**CULINARY TIP**
Salmon is a rich source of Omega-3 fatty acids, which are
beneficial in the prevention of heart disease.

**HOW I RATE THIS SUSHI**

# CALIFORNIA ROLL

## CALIFORNIA ROLL

| | |
|---|---|
| Crab | Mayonnaise |
| Avocado | Rice |
| Cucumber | Nori |
| Smelt roe | |

**IF YOU LIKE CALIFORNIA ROLL, TRY**
ALASKA, SPIDER ROLL

---

**AT THE SUSHI BAR**
Each place at the sushi bar is marked by a small saucer and
a pair of hashi or chopsticks, with or without a ceramic
holder, a hashi oki. Unwrap your hashi and separate them.
When you're not using them, they belong directly in front
of you, parallel with the edge of the counter.

HOW I RATE
THIS SUSHI

# CHIRASHIZUSHI

## CHIRASHIZUSHI

| | |
|---|---|
| Assorted sashimi | Wasabi |
| Shiitake mushroom | Rice |
| Kampyo | Nori |

## IF YOU LIKE CHIRASHIZUSHI, TRY
*BARAZUSHI*

## A LESSON IN JAPANESE
*Sushi Tsu.*
True aficionados. Those who love to eat sushi.

### HOW I RATE THIS SUSHI

# EBI

## SHRIMP

Shrimp
Wasabi
Rice

### IF YOU LIKE EBI, TRY
AMA-EBI, KANI, *SHAKO*

### A LESSON IN JAPANESE
*Sumimasen*.
Excuse me.

HOW I RATE
THIS SUSHI

# FUGU
## BLOWFISH

| Blowfish | (Green onion) |
| Wasabi | (Radish) |
| Rice | |

## IF YOU LIKE FUGU, TRY
HIRAME, TAI, SUZUKI

### CULINARY TIP
*Fugu must be prepared with the utmost care because its organs,
mainly the guts, contain a deadly poison. Fugu is a great
delicacy, and is available only in winter.*

**HOW I RATE
THIS SUSHI**

# FUTOMAKI

## FUTOMAKI

| Omelet | Sea eel (and/or shrimp) |
| Kampyo | Rice |
| Shiitake mushroom | Nori |
| Fish powder | |

### IF YOU LIKE FUTOMAKI, TRY
KAMPYO MAKI, TAMAGO

### CULINARY TIP
Generally, maki-zushi and temaki should be eaten first, since the crisp nori can get soggy after touching the damp rice.

HOW I RATE
THIS SUSHI

# HAMACHI
## YELLOW TAIL TUNA

Yellow tail tuna
Rice
Wasabi

## IF YOU LIKE HAMACHI, TRY
*HIRAMASA, KAMPACHI, SHIMAAJI*

## A LESSON IN JAPANESE
*Kanpai!*
Cheers!

### HOW I RATE
THIS SUSHI

# HIRAME
## FLOUNDER

Flounder
Rice
Wasabi

## IF YOU LIKE HIRAME, TRY
FUGU, SUZUKI, TAI

## A LESSON IN JAPANESE
*O genki desuka?*
How are you? (polite form)

### HOW I RATE THIS SUSHI

# HOKKIGAI
## SURF CLAM

Surf clam
Rice
Wasabi
Nori

**IF YOU LIKE HOKKIGAI, TRY**
*AKAGAI, AOYAGI, TORIGAI*

### AT THE SUSHI BAR
The waitress will ask you what you want to drink and
whether you would like a bowl of soup. Ask her for sake,
tea, or beer, but order your sashimi or sushi directly from
the chef. It is not considered polite to ask the chef for
drinks or other food than sushi or sashimi.

HOW I RATE
THIS SUSHI

# HOTATEGAI
## SCALLOP

| | |
|---|---|
| Scallop | (Lemon juice) |
| Rice | (Nori) |
| Wasabi | |

## IF YOU LIKE HOTATEGAI, TRY
*KOBASHIRA*, MIRUGAI, *TAIRAGI*

## A LESSON IN JAPANESE
*Konnichiwa!*
Hello!

### HOW I RATE THIS SUSHI

# IKA
# SQUID

Squid
Rice
Wasabi

## IF YOU LIKE IKA, TRY
*AWABI*, TAKO

## JAPANESE ETIQUETTE
The soup will be served in a covered bowl to keep it hot.
Remove the cover, pick up the bowl in one hand, pick out
the solid bits with your chopsticks, then drink the broth
like tea. Don't worry about slurping. It's considered
perfectly proper.

## HOW I RATE THIS SUSHI

# IKURA
## SALMON ROE

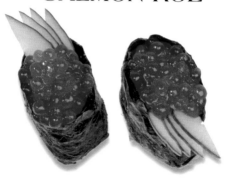

| | |
|---|---|
| Salmon roe | Nori |
| Rice | Cucumber |
| Wasabi | |

## IF YOU LIKE IKURA, TRY
MASAGO, RISING SUN, TOBIKO, UNI

### A LESSON IN JAPANESE
The name ikura is derived from "ikra," the Russian word for fish roe or caviar. This is why ikura is sometimes used as red caviar in American cuisine, as well as in sushi.

HOW I RATE
THIS SUSHI

# INARI ZUSHI
## TOFU POCKET

Tofu (deep fried and marinated)
Rice
Sesame seeds

### IF YOU LIKE INARI ZUSHI, TRY
FUTOMAKI, KAMPYO

### AT THE SUSHI BAR
Sushi chefs are often enthusiastic and helpful in recommending the best selections. Novice sushi addicts and experienced eaters alike should feel free to ask the chef for advice and recommendations. This demonstrates respect for the chef, who will give you the best pieces.

### HOW I RATE THIS SUSHI

# IWASHI
## SARDINE

Sardine
Rice
Wasabi

Ginger
(Green onion)

## IF YOU LIKE IWASHI, TRY
AJI, KOHADA, SABA

### A LESSON IN JAPANESE
*Omakase.*
Asking the sushi chef to choose
what you'll have next.

**HOW I RATE THIS SUSHI**

# KAMIKAZE

## KAMIKAZE

| | |
|---|---|
| Tempura flakes | Spicy sauce |
| Avocado | Rice |
| Cucumber | Nori |
| Salmon | |

**IF YOU LIKE KAMIKAZE, TRY**
SNAKE (see page 5), *DYNAMITE MAKI*

**A LESSON IN JAPANESE:**
*Arigato gozaimas*
Thank you very much (formal)

HOW I RATE THIS SUSHI

| 1 | 2 | 3 | 4 | 5 |
|---|---|---|---|---|

# KAMPYO
# FLOWER ROOTS

Flower roots
Rice
Wasabi
Nori

## IF YOU LIKE KAMPYO, TRY
INARI ZUSHI

## A LESSON IN JAPANESE
*Itadakimasu!*
Let's eat! (Literally meaning: "I gratefully receive.")

HOW I RATE
THIS SUSHI

# KANI
## SNOW CRAB

Snow crab
Rice
Wasabi
(Lemon juice)

**IF YOU LIKE KANI, TRY**
CALIFORNIA ROLL, EBI, KANI-KAMA

**A LESSON IN JAPANESE**
*Konbanwa.*
Good evening.

**HOW I RATE THIS SUSHI**

# KANI-KAMA
## CRAB STICK

Crab
Rice
Wasabi
Nori

### IF YOU LIKE KANI-KAMA, TRY
CALIFORNIA ROLL, KANI

### JAPANESE ETIQUETTE
Pour a little soy sauce into your saucer and use it for
dipping the sushi, remembering that the shoyu is intended
to season the fish, not the rice. Soaking sushi in soy sauce
obscures the flavours and causes the rice pad
to disintegrate.

HOW I RATE
THIS SUSHI

# KAPPA MAKI

## CUCUMBER ROLL

| Cucumber | Nori |
| --- | --- |
| Rice | Sesame seeds |
| Wasabi | |

### IF YOU LIKE KAPPA MAKI, TRY
AVOCADO, OSHINKO MAKI

### A LESSON IN JAPANESE
Also called Kyuri. The name refers to a mythological goblin who was fond of the vegetable. It is rolled in sesame seeds to enhance the flavour.

HOW I RATE
THIS SUSHI

# KAZUNOKO
## HERRING ROE

| | |
|---|---|
| Herring roe (marinated) | Nori |
| Bonito flake | (Sea kelp) |
| Rice | |

**IF YOU LIKE KAZUNOKO, TRY**
MASAGO, TOBIKO

---

**SUSHI ETIQUETTE**
At the Sushi bar, when you're finished, ask the waitress -
not the chef - for the bill, Oaiso. The chef will add up and
give it to the waitress, who will bring it to you and take
your money. In Japanese restaurants, people who handle
food never handle money, and vice versa.

**HOW I RATE THIS SUSHI**

# KUNSEI SYAKE

## SMOKED SALMON

| | |
|---|---|
| Smoked salmon | (Lemon) |
| Rice | (Radish sprouts) |
| Wasabi | |

**IF YOU LIKE KUNSEI SYAKE, TRY**
BENI JAKE, SYAKE

**TRAVELERS**
Sushi is the perfect airborne picnic, light and
easy to digest.

HOW I RATE
THIS SUSHI

| 1 | 2 | 3 | 4 | 5 |
|---|---|---|---|---|

# KOHADA

## GRIZZARD SHAD

| Grizzard shad | (Ginger) |
| Rice | (Green onion) |
| Wasabi | |

## IF YOU LIKE KOHADA, TRY
AJI, *MAMAKARI, SAYORI*

## A LESSON IN JAPANESE
*Oishii!*
Delicious!

HOW I RATE
THIS SUSHI

# MAGURO

## RED TUNA

Red tuna
Rice
Wasabi

**IF YOU LIKE MAGURO, TRY**
*KAJIKI MAGURO, KATSUO,* SHIRO MAGURO,
TORO

**SUSHI ETIQUETTE**
As you are seated, a waitress will bring you an oshibori, a
hot towel. Use it to wipe your hands, then fold it and put it
back on the counter or in the basket. A regular napkin will
be provided for your lap.

**HOW I RATE THIS SUSHI**

# MASAGO
## SMELT ROE

Smelt Roe
Rice
Wasabi
Nori

### IF YOU LIKE MASAGO, TRY
IKURA, KAZUNOKO, RISING SUN, TOBIKO

### AT THE SUSHI BAR
Masago is rich in Omega-3 fatty acids, which are beneficial for preventing heart disease.

### HOW I RATE THIS SUSHI

# MIRUGAI
## KING CLAM

King clam
Rice
Wasabi
Nori

## IF YOU LIKE MIRUGAI, TRY
*AKAGAI, AWABI*

## A LESSON IN JAPANESE
*Ika o kudasai*
Please give me squid
*Maguro o kudasai*
Please give me tuna

**HOW I RATE THIS SUSHI**

# NEGI HAMACHI
## YELLOW TAIL TUNA

| | |
|---|---|
| Yellow tail tuna | Wasabi |
| Chopped shallots | Nori |
| Rice | |

## IF YOU LIKE NEGI HAMACHI, TRY
TEKKA MAKI, *TORO TEKKA*

### A LESSON IN JAPANESE
In Japan, every sushi shop has its own house sauce, darker and thicker than regular soy sauce, known as murasaki, which means "purple."

HOW I RATE
THIS SUSHI

# NEGI HAMACHI TEMAKI
## YELLOW TAIL TUNA

| | |
|---|---|
| Yellow tail tuna | Rice |
| Green onion | Wasabi |
| Cucumber | Nori |
| Sesame seeds | |

**IF YOU LIKE NEGI HAMA TEMAKI, TRY**
*KAMPACHI, SHIMAAJI*

**SUSHI ETIQUETTE**
When you place the sushi in your mouth, do it
so that the fish hits your taste buds.

**HOW I RATE THIS SUSHI**

# OSHINKO MAKI
## OSHINKO MAKI

| | |
|---|---|
| Pickle | Rice |
| Radish | Nori |
| Sesame seeds | |

## IF YOU LIKE OSHINKO MAKI, TRY
KAPPA MAKI, *UMESHISO*

### AT THE SUSHI BAR
The most skilful sushi chefs even tailor the size of each sushi finger to the mouth of the person who is about to eat it.

HOW I RATE
THIS SUSHI

# PHILADELPHIA
## PHILADELPHIA

| | |
|---|---|
| Smoked salmon | Masago |
| Cream cheese | Rice |
| Cucumber | Nori |
| Lettuce | |

### IF YOU LIKE PHILADELPHIA, TRY
ALASKA, CALIFORNIA ROLL

---

### SUSHI ETIQUETTE
There is a ritual involved in the drinking of sake, starting
with pouring the first drink for someone else.

HOW I RATE
THIS SUSHI

1  2  3  4  5

# RISING SUN

## SCALLOP AND TOBIKO

| Scallop | Rice |
|---------|------|
| Quail egg | Nori |
| Tobiko | |

## IF YOU LIKE RISING SUN, TRY
IKURA, MASAGO, TOBIKO

### A LESSON IN JAPANESE
*Domo arigato.*
Thank you very much.

HOW I RATE
THIS SUSHI

# SABA
## OILY MACKEREL

Oily mackerel
Rice
Wasabi

**IF YOU LIKE SABA, TRY**
AJI, IWASHI, *SAWARA*

**SUSHI ETIQUETTE**
Don't drown your sushi. Shoyu is intended to complement,
not overwhelm, the flavour of sushi, and the purpose is to
flavour the fish, not the rice.

HOW I RATE
THIS SUSHI

# SALMON SKIN
## GRILLED SALMON SKIN

| | |
|---|---|
| Grilled salmon skin | Rice |
| Radish sprouts | Sesame seeds |
| Nitsume (sweet sauce) | Tobiko |
| Nori | |

### IF YOU LIKE SALMON SKIN, TRY
UNA-KYU, UNAGI

### SUSHI ETIQUETTE
The main thing to remember about wasabi is that it's very
hot and spicy. So be careful and use only a tiny, tiny dab:
you don't want to overwhelm the taste of the fish
or the topping.

### HOW I RATE THIS SUSHI

# SHIRO MAGURO
## ALBACORE

Albacore
Rice
Wasabi

### IF YOU LIKE SHIRO MAGURO, TRY
HAMACHI, MAGURO, TORO

### SUSHI ETIQUETTE
Chopsticks are de rigueur for sashimi and maki-zushi, but
nigiri-zushi (hand-rolled sushi) is considered finger food.

### HOW I RATE
THIS SUSHI

| 1 | 2 | 3 | 4 | 5 |
|---|---|---|---|---|
| ✓ | ☺ | ☺ | ☺ | ☺ | ☺ |

# SPICY TUNA MAKI
## SPICY TUNA

| | |
|---|---|
| Tuna | Spicy sauce |
| Cucumber | Rice |
| Tobiko | Nori |
| Radish sprouts | |

### IF YOU LIKE SPICY TUNA MAKI, TRY
*SPICY SALMON, SPICY SCALLOPS*

### SUSHI ETIQUETTE
One bite or two? That depends on the size of the sushi,
which tends to be bigger in North America.

HOW I RATE
THIS SUSHI

# SPICY TUNA GUNKAN
## SPICY TUNA

| | |
|---|---|
| Spicy tuna | Nori |
| Flying fish roe | Green onion |
| Rice | |

### IF YOU LIKE SPICY TUNA GUNKAN, TRY
*SPICY SALMON, SPICY SCALLOPS*

### A LESSON IN JAPANESE
*Kyo wa nani ga oishii desu ka ?*
What is good today?

HOW I RATE
THIS SUSHI

# SPIDER ROLL

## SPIDER ROLL

| | |
|---|---|
| Softshell crab | Masago |
| Avocado | Mayonnaise |
| Cucumber | Rice |
| Lettuce | Nori |
| Bonito flake | |

## IF YOU LIKE SPIDER ROLL, TRY
ALASKA, *TEMPURA ROLL*

## SUSHI ETIQUETTE
When you pick up a delectable morsel from a friend's plate, make sure you turn your chopsticks around and use the other end.

## HOW I RATE THIS SUSHI

| 1 | 2 | 3 | 4 | 5 |
|---|---|---|---|---|
| ✓ | ☹ | 😐 | 🙂 | 😊 |

# SUZUKI

## SEA BASS

Sea bass
Rice
Wasabi

**IF YOU LIKE SUZUKI, TRY**
HIRAME, TAI

**SUSHI ETIQUETTE**
It is recommended not to drink hard liquor,
which anaesthetizes the taste buds.

HOW I RATE
THIS SUSHI

# SYAKE
## ATLANTIC SALMON

Atlantic salmon
Rice
Wasabi

### IF YOU LIKE SYAKE, TRY
BENI JAKE, *KAJIKI MAGURO*

### A LESSON IN JAPANESE
Syake, salmon, is not to be confused with sake, rice wine.

HOW I RATE
THIS SUSHI

# SYAKE MAKI

## SALMON

Salmon
Rice
Wasabi
Nori

**IF YOU LIKE SYAKE MAKI, TRY**
BENI JAKE, SYAKE, TEKKA MAKI

**SUSHI ETIQUETTE**
Gari is essential for refreshing your palate between bites of
different types of sushi. Think of it as a palate cleanser, like
the sorbet served between courses at gourmet restaurants.

HOW I RATE
THIS SUSHI

# TAI

## RED SNAPPER

Red snapper
Rice
Wasabi

**IF YOU LIKE TAI, TRY**
HIRAME, SUZUKI

**CULINARY TIP**
The fish the Japanese call tai is not available in North America. Red snapper, also known as porgy, is what goes by the name of tai in sushi bars here.

HOW I RATE
THIS SUSHI

# TAKO
## OCTOPUS

Octopus
Rice
Wasabi
Nori

**IF YOU LIKE TAKO, TRY**
IKA

**CULINARY TIP**
Tako is always boiled before serving, which tenderizes the flesh and leaves the meat with a subtle, slightly chewy texture.

HOW I RATE
THIS SUSHI

# TAMAGO
## EGG CLUSTER

Omelet
Rice
Nori

## IF YOU LIKE TAMAGO, TRY
FUTOMAKI

## A LESSON IN JAPANESE
This rolled egg omelette is also known as Gyoku,
which means "jewel".

## HOW I RATE
THIS SUSHI

# TEKKA MAKI
## TUNA ROLLS

Tuna
Rice
Wasabi
Nori

**IF YOU LIKE TEKKA MAKI, TRY**
MAGURO, NEGI HAMACHI, SYAKE MAKI, *SPICY HAMACHI*, TORO

---

**A LESSON IN JAPANESE**
The name tekka literally means "iron fire". It got its name because the bright red fresh tuna in the middle reminded people of a red-hot iron bar.

---

**HOW I RATE THIS SUSHI**

# TOBIKO
## FLYING FISH ROE

Flying fish roe
Rice
Nori

### IF YOU LIKE TOBIKO, TRY
IKURA, MASAGO, RISING SUN

### SUSHI ETIQUETTE
Green tea, usually called ocha, brings out the flavour of
sushi, removes any aftertastes, and freshens the mouth for
the next serving.

HOW I RATE
THIS SUSHI

| 1 | 2 | 3 | 4 | 5 |
|---|---|---|---|---|
| ✓ | ☺ | ☺ | ☺ | ☺ |

# TORO
## FATTY TUNA

Tuna (belly)
Rice
Wasabi

**IF YOU LIKE TORO, TRY**
*BINCHO MAGURO, NEGI TORO MAKI*

**CULINARY TIP**
Part of the Tuna's belly. Fatty. It is considered
a great delicacy.

**HOW I RATE THIS SUSHI**

| 1 | 2 | 3 | 4 | 5 |
| --- | --- | --- | --- | --- |

# UME-KYU
## UME-KYU

| | |
|---|---|
| Cucumber | Rice |
| Shiso leaves | Nori |
| Ume (plumpaste) | |

**IF YOU LIKE UME-KYU, TRY**
KAPPA MAKI

**AT THE SUSHI BAR**
Shokunin, or sushi chefs, perform behind the counter, standing atop a raised platform.

HOW I RATE
THIS SUSHI

# UNA-KYU

## GRILLED EEL

| | |
|---|---|
| Grilled eel | Nori |
| Cucumber | Rice |
| Tare | Sesame seeds |

## IF YOU LIKE UNA-KYU, TRY
ANAGO, SALMON SKIN, UNAGI

### CULINARY TIP
The flat green plastic garnish shaped like a picket fence is called a Baran. It harks back to the ancient tradition of wrapping fish in parts of the bamboo plant that contained natural preservatives to keep the fish fresh. As refrigeration became widely available, this was no longer necessary.

### HOW I RATE THIS SUSHI

# UNAGI
## FRESH WATER EEL

Fresh water eel
Rice
Tare
Nori

**IF YOU LIKE UNAGI, TRY**
ANAGO, SALMON SKIN, UNA-KYU

**CULINARY TIP**
Unagi is grilled, then glazed with a mixture of soy sauce, sugar, and eel broth. The sauce makes it taste sweet and rich. It should be eaten without any dipping sauce.

HOW I RATE
THIS SUSHI

# UNI

## SEA URCHIN ROE

Sea urchin roe
Rice
Nori

**IF YOU LIKE UNI, TRY**
IKURA

---

**CULINARY TIP**
Uni is considered a great delicacy. Soft in texture, it has a delicious, subtle, nutlike flavor.

HOW I RATE THIS SUSHI

# ■THE ESSENTIALS

The Sushi experience introduces you to a whole new language. The following is an abbreviated list of some of the basic Japanese words you may hear or read at sushi bars and restaurants.

## ABURA AGE
Deep-fried bean curd.

## AGARI
Hot green tea, usually called ocha. Agari (a sushi slang term) signifies that you have finished eating. Originally, agari meant only the cup of tea served after the meal, but now it can refer to tea consumed at any point in the meal. It is always taken clear, without milk or sugar, and piping hot. It is perfectly acceptable to slurp your tea.

## AKAMI
The flesh around the spine of tuna, which is red and lean.

## AMBERJACK
(See HAMACHI)

## ANAGO
Marine eel, a leaner version of unagi, freshwater eel, is always boiled first, then grilled. Because it is served with a special mixture of sugar, soy sauce and eel stock, no dipping sauce or wasabi is needed.
(See "On the menu," page 21.)

## AVOCADO
A pear-shaped fruit grown in Mexico, the West Indies, Florida and California. The flesh, an attractive shade of pale green, is used in the preparation of maki sushi.

## AWABI
Abalone, a sea snail much prized for its mother-of-pearl inner shell and the subtle flavour of its edible "foot." For sushi, it is sliced across the grain and scored slightly to tenderize it and give the soy sauce something to stick to.

## AWASEZU
(See KOMEZU)

## BAMBOO MAT
(See MAKISU)

## BARAN
A flat green plastic garnish shaped like a picket fence. Purely decorative, it is not meant to be eaten! It harks back to the ancient tradition of wrapping fish in parts of the bamboo plant that contained natural preservatives to keep the fish fresh. As refrigeration became widely available, this was no longer necessary.

## BIIRU
Beer is an excellent accompaniment to sushi and sashimi. Among the Japanese beers served in sushi bars, Kirin has a rich, nutlike flavour, Asahi is the sweetest, and Sapporo is lighter but more bitter.

## BOSTON ROLL
A type of maki sushi made with scallion, crab, and salmon.

## CALIFORNIA ROLL
Very popular with beginning sushi eaters, California rolls are hand rolls made of cooked crabmeat, avocado and cucumber. (See "On the menu," page 24.)

# ■THE ESSENTIALS

## CAVIAR (RED)
*(See IKURA)*

## CHIRASHIZUSHI
The name means "scattered sushi." Sushi rice is served
in a bowl or box, decorated with nine types of toppings
(the Japanese consider nine the luckiest number), such
as sliced raw fish, cooked vegetables or rolled omelette.
*(See "On the menu," page 25.)*

## CRAB
*(See KANI)*

## CUCUMBER
*(See KYURI)*

## DAIKON
Japanese radish, large, white, juicy and crisp. Rich in
Vitamin C, daikon is used in salads or as a garnish.

## DASHI
A clear, non-oily fish stock used to make soup, salad
dressings and marinades. Dashi can be based on kombu,
katsuoboshi and/or dried shiitake mushrooms.

## EBI
Sweet, fresh-tasting ebi are jumbo shrimp (prawns) that
are boiled in salted water, then shelled and spread into
butterfly shape, leaving only the shell of the tails
attached. They are usually eaten with wasabi and soy
sauce. *(See "On the menu," page 26.)*

## EDAMAME

Fresh green soybean pods with the beans still inside, sometimes presented by the chef as a tsukidashi or side dish. Considered a great delicacy in Japan, often served with a glass of ice-cold beer, edamame are rich in protein, Vitamin A, and several B vitamins, as well as calcium and Vitamin C.

## FISH ROE
*(See IKURA)*

## FLOUNDER
*(See HIRAME)*

## FLYING FISH ROE
*(See TOBIKO)*

## FUKUSA-ZUSHI

A "parcel" of omelette folded around vinegared rice and smoked fish.

## FUTO MAKI

Fat, rolled *sushi*, usually made with five different seasoned ingredients.

## GARI

Tender young ginger root pickled in salt and sweetened vinegar, a garnish used to freshen the palate between different types of sushi. It has antibacterial properties, aids in digestion, and helps reinforce the body's defences against colds and flu.

## GINGER
*(See GARI)*

# ■THE ESSENTIALS

## GOBOU
Mountain burdock, a root vegetable with a sweet, nutty flavour and crunchy texture, is very rich in dietary fibre.

## GOHANMONO
Age rice used for *sushi*.

## GOMA
Sesame seeds, which can be either black or white, are frequently used in rolled sushi for colour and flavour.

## GREEN TEA
*(See AGARI and SENCHA)*

## GUNKAN
Known as "boat-style" sushi, gunkan is a type of nigiri-zushi that is made by wrapping a band of seaweed around a pad of rice and pressing down so the ingredients lie on top. This is an easy way to serve fish roe and other smaller ingredients.

## GYOKU
Rolled egg omelette, also known as *tamago*. G*yoku* means "jewel". (*see* TAMAGO)

## HAKO ZUSHI
Boxed of pressed *sushi*, prepared in a special pressing box to create finger-shaped blocks of *sushi*.

## HAMACHI
Hamachi is a variety of yellowtail tuna, which is the common name for amberjack. It is light yellow in colour and has a rich smooth smoky taste. Sushi chefs consider the tail and the cheek of the fish the best parts, which they often save and cook for special customers. (*See "On the menu," page 29.*)

## HANGIRI
A container made of unfinished cypress wood, used for mixing cooked sushi rice with vinegar dressing.

## HASHI
Chopsticks. Even if you are uncoordinated, you should try to use them. (Forks and knives are seldom found at sushi bars, and using them is considered an insult to the chef. It is fine to use your fingers to pick up sushi, but not sashimi.) When you taste something from a friend's dish, turn your chopsticks around and use the other end.

## HASHI OKI
Chopstick holders, found at each place in a sushi restaurant.

## HIRAME
Flounder, a flat fish that makes excellent sashimi, cut into paper-thin, transparent slices.
*(See "On the menu," page 30.)*

## HORSERADISH
*(See WASABI)*

## HOSOMAKI
*(See MAKI SUSHI)*

## IKA
Squid, an exotic member of the shellfish family that has no outer shell. The flesh is pearly white and glossy. The firm, flat flesh is sliced and scored slightly to tenderize it and give the soy sauce something to cling to.
*(See "On the menu," page 33.)*

# ■THE ESSENTIALS

## IKURA
Salmon roe, red shiny ball-like sushi. The name ikura is derived from "ikra," the Russian word for fish roe or caviar. This is why ikura is sometimes used as red caviar in American cuisine, as well as in sushi. Ikura is never eaten raw due to the risk of parasites.
*(See "On the menu," page 34.)*

## INARI ZUSHI
Golden sweet sushi, made of rice packed in fried thin tofu that is simmered in a sweet liquid.

## ITAMAE-SAN
*(See SHOKUNIN)*

## JAPANESE SHAD
*(See KOHADA)*

## KAMPYO
Flower roots.

## KANI
Real crab meat, used for certain types of sushi. Always served cooked, kani is an excellent choice for sushi novices. It can be enjoyed as nigiri-zushi or wrapped in seaweed, as in California rolls.
*(See "On the menu," page 39.)*

## KAPPA MAKI
Rolled sushi made with Japanese cucumber. The name refers to a mythological goblin who was fond of the vegetable. *(See "On the menu," page 41.)*

## KARASHI
Japanese hot mustard, sold in tubes or powder.

## KATSUOBUSHI
Bonito flakes. The dried form of bonito fish, used as a stock base to make delicious, nutritious soups, is rich in minerals, vitamins, and protein.

## KELP
(See KOMBU)

## KOHADA
A marinated Japanese fish with silvery skin, similar to a sardine, used as a topping on *nigiri-zushi*.

## KOMBU
Kelp, a tall, leafy plant that grows in shallow water. It provides iodine, vitamins, protein and dietary fibre. It also contains chemicals that can fight high cholesterol, high blood pressure, and perhaps some forms of cancer.

## KYURI
Japanese cucumber. Unlike the cucumbers grown here, the Japanese variety has tiny bumps all over the skins and fewer seeds inside. The texture is very crisp.

## MACKEREL
(See SABA)

## MAGURO
Tuna. Maguro is the most popular item sold at sushi bars in North America, due to its familiarity and fresh, clean taste. Although there are many varieties of tuna, yellowfin or bluefin lean cut tuna is what is used for sushi. (See "On the menu," page 45.)

# ■THE ESSENTIALS

## MAKI-ZUSHI
Also spelled maki-zushi. Rolled sushi, made by wrapping rice, fish, and other ingredients into a long seaweed roll, which is then sliced into bite-sized pieces. There are two types of maki-zushi rolls: hosomaki, a slender roll cut into six small pieces, and temaki, a hand roll eaten in two or three bites that looks like an ice cream cone. Maki-zushi is served with soy sauce and gari. Maki-zushi is said to have originated in eighteenth-century gambling houses in Japan, where gamers wanted something easy to eat while gambling.

## MAKISU
Used for preparing maki-zushi, a makisu is a mat made from bamboo sticks tied together with cotton string.

## MASAGO
Smelt roe. Masago are small orange flying fish eggs, a prized delicacy in Japan. Masago can be prepared as nigiri-zushi, gunkan or maki-zushi and is often used for garnishing the outside of hand rolls. It is closely related to tobiko, a flying fish roe, and though slightly lighter in colour, has a similar taste, salty and resistant to the bite. It is rich in Omega-3 fatty acids, which are beneficial for preventing heart disease.
(See "On the menu," page 46.)

## MASU-ZUSHI
A form of *oshi-zushi* or pressed *sushi*, made with a thin slice of smoked salmon or trout pressed onto a finger of rice.

## MIRIN
Japanese sweet rice wine, used only for cooking.

## MIRUGAI

Geoduck (pronounced "gooey-duck"), a large hardshell clam that can be well over a foot long with its thick "neck." Slightly elastic to the bite, it is sliced thin for sushi or sashimi and sometimes fringed on the edges for decorative appeal and tenderness.
*(See "On the menu," page 47.)*

## MISO

Fermented soybean paste, mixed with dashi fish stock to make soup. The rule of thumb is the darker the colour, the saltier the taste. Miso, which is highly nutritious, is also used in marinades, dressings and sauces.

## MURASAKI

*(See SHOYU)*

## MUSHROOM

*(See SHIITAKE)*

## NAMIDA

Literally "tears" - another term for *wasabi* that makes your eyes water.

## NIGIRI-ZUSHI

Also spelled nigiri sushi. Meaning "pressed by hand," nigiri-zushi is a slice of cooked or uncooked fish lying across a pad of rice. The ingredients are then gently pressed together. Fish roe is also made into nigiri-zushi, in which case a strip of nori is wrapped around to hold it together. Nigiri-zushi is often served with wasabi and dipped in soy sauce.

# ■THE ESSENTIALS

**NORI**
The seaweed used to wrap sushi. Nori is rich in iodine and iron and extremely high in Vitamins A, $B_1$, $B_2$, $B_6$, Niacin and Vitamin C.

**NORI MAKI**
Simple rolled *sushi*, made from rice spread on nori with various fillings, rolled up and cut into slices.

**OCHA**
(*See* AGARI)

**OCTOPUS**
(*See* TAKO)

**OSHIBORI**
The hot towel given to diners so they can wipe their hands before eating.

**OSHINKO**
Pale yellow pickled daikon radish.

**OSHIWAKU**
A wooden box used as a large mould for pressed *sushi*.

**OSHI-ZUSHI**
Pressed *sushi*, made in a special mould or box.

**OTEMOTO**
Chopsticks, used for all kinds of Japanese dishes, except soup.

**PHILADELPHIA ROLL**
Another non-traditional form of maki sushi, made with smoked salmon, cream cheese, and cucumber.
(*See* "On the menu," *page* 51.)

## RED SNAPPER
*(See TAI)*

## RICE
*(See SHARI)*

## SABA
Mackerel. Rich in Omega-3 fatty acids, this fish is salted and marinated up to nine hours before being served. *(See "On the menu," page 53.)*

## SAKE
Japanese rice wine is the national alcoholic beverage. Made from fermented rice, sake is served warm before the meal, not during or after. Some consider the drink obligatory, while others say it's redundant because, like sushi, it is made from rice. Remember, the waiter will continue to fill an empty cup, so turn it over when you're done. (And yes, it is acceptable to drink sake with sashimi, which is not made with rice.)

## SALMON
*(See SYAKE)*

## SASHIMI
Fresh raw seafood fillets cut into bite-sized oblong strips, dipped in shoyu and eaten with wasabi and gari. Sashimi is carefully selected from the purest waters and prepared by specially trained sashimi chefs to ensure the highest quality. Sashimi is generally eaten at the beginning of the meal, before the sushi. The most popular types of fish used for sashimi are maguro (tuna), hamachi (yellowtail tuna), saba (mackerel), flounder and sea bream.

## SEA BASS
*(See SUZUKI)*

# ■THE ESSENTIALS

**SEA EEL**
(*See* ANAGO)

**SEA URCHIN**
(*See* UNI)

**SEAWEED**
(*See* NORI)

**SENCHA**
The best-quality green tea, made from the first harvest.
It has a pleasantly bitter flavour and a lovely light-green
colour. Sencha tastes especially good with raw fish.

**SESAME SEEDS**
(*See* GOMA)

**SHAMOJI**
The broad wooden paddle used in Japan to mix sushi
rice and aerate the rice so that it cools quickly. A paper
fan or even a folded newspaper can be used to cool the
rice.

**SHARI**
The name for sushi rice, shari, is derived from a
Sanskrit word. Rice is the foundation of sushi. It is
steamed, then tossed in a dressing of rice vinegar, sugar,
and salt, while an assistant stands by, fanning the rice to
cool it quickly. It takes years to master the process and
achieve the chewiness and glossy sheen so prized by
sushi lovers, and then to learn how to form the rice
into pads exactly the right consistency and size for
nigiri-zushi. Prepared sushi rice is stored at cool room
temperature, covered with a damp cloth. It should
never be refrigerated, or the texture will become
unpleasantly firm.

## SHIITAKE
Shiitake (mushrooms) are available both fresh and dried.
They are in season in spring and fall, and are grown
commercially in large quantities by inoculating cut logs
of the Shii tree and other oak-related species with spores.

## SHISO
An aromatic herb from the mint family, with pretty,
serrated leaves. A red-leafed variety is used to flavour
and colour umeboshi and various pickled vegetables.

## SHOGA
Ginger, one of the most ancient seasonings, was
originally brought from China to Japan. Pickled ginger,
known as gari, is thin-sliced young ginger pickled in sugar
and vinegar. The vinegar is what gives the ginger its pale
pink colour. Ginger has antiseptic properties.

## SHOKUNIN
Traditional master sushi chef. Also called Itamae-san.
Sushi chefs are true artists who undergo long, hard years
of apprenticeship before being allowed to venture out
on their own. Sushi chefs perform behind the counter,
standing atop a raised platform. They are often
enthusiastic and helpful in recommending the best
selections. Novice sushi addicts and experienced eaters
alike should feel free to ask the chef for advice and
recommendations. This demonstrates respect for the
chef, who will give you the best pieces.

## SHOYU
Soy sauce. Shoyu is both an ingredient and a
condiment. The darker sauce is thicker and often less salty
than the lighter one. There are also low-sodium varieties.
Japanese soy sauce is naturally fermented and less salty
than Chinese soy sauce, which makes it more appropriate
as a dipping sauce for sushi. At a sushi restaurant,
aficionados ask for "murasaki" (purple), rather than shoyu.

# ■THE ESSENTIALS

**SHRIMP**
*(See EBI)*

**SMELT ROE**
*(See MASAGO)*

**SOBA ZUSHI**
A novelty dish made with soba noodles that is very popular in Japan. Cooked noodles with a filling are rolled in nori and cut into bite-sized disks. Soba zushi is served with a special dipping sauce instead of shoyu.

**SOY SAUCE**
*(See SHOYU)*

**SU**
*Sushi* vinegar, a special blend of rice vinegar, sugar and salt used to make *sushi* rice.

**SUIMONO**
Clear Japanese soup.

**SUMESHI**
Vinegared rice, made by tossing freshly cooked rice with rice vinegar, sugar and salt.

**SUSHI**
A Japanese staple that combines vinegar-flavoured rice with fish. Sushi comes in many forms and can be eaten with hashi (chopsticks) or with your hands. The most common types of sushi are nigiri-zushi (handmade sushi) and maki-zushi (rolled sushi made with a bamboo mat).

**SUSHI CHEF**
*(See SHOKUNIN)*

**SUSHI TSU**
True aficionados - those who love to eat sushi.

## SUZUKI

Sea bass, a mild-flavoured Japanese fish with shiny white flesh. Sometimes served as sashimi and called suzuki usu zukuri. *(See "On the menu," page 59.)*

## SYAKE

Salmon (not to be confused with sake, rice wine). A very popular kind of sushi, easily recognizable by its bright orange colour and sweet, tender flavour. In sushi bars, salmon is always served marinated or smoked, which gives it a sweet, somewhat smoky taste. Fresh grilled salmon is sometimes presented as nigiri zushi. Salmon is a rich source of Omega-3 fatty acids, which are beneficial in the prevention of heart disease.
*(See "On the menu," page 60.)*

## TAI

The fish the Japanese call tai is not available in North America. Red snapper, also known as porgy, is what goes by the name of tai in sushi bars here. Both are sweet, lean fish with pink-and-white flesh.
*(See "On the menu," page 62.)*

## TAKO

Octopus, easily recognized by its burgundy tentacles; in fact, the legs of the octopus are actually more commonly eaten than the body. Tako is always boiled before serving, which tenderizes the flesh and leaves the meat with a subtle flavour and slightly chewy texture.
*(See "On the menu," page 63.)*

# ■THE ESSENTIALS

## TAKO BUTSU
Chunk-style octopus.

## TAKUAN
Pickled *daikon* radish, used as a garnish.

## TAMAGO
A firm omelette made in a square pan from sweetened egg batter. It is cooled, sliced and served as sushi on a pad of rice with a narrow belt of nori or tucked into a sushi roll. (*See "On the menu", page 64*)

## TAMARI
A sauce used for dipping.

## TANE
Topping ingredients used for *nigiri-zushi*.

## TARE
Sweet sauce.

## TEKKA MAKI
A thin rolled sushi with a block of maguro tuna in the centre. The name tekka literally means "iron fire." It got its name because the bright red fresh tuna in the middle reminded people of a red-hot iron bar. It can be made with or without wasabi.
(*See "On the menu", page 65*)

## TEMAKI-ZUSHI
Literally, hand-rolled sushi, a variation of maki-zushi. The temaki is a large cone-shaped roll (similar to an ice cream cone), which usually contains larger items, such as pieces of vegetables and smoked salmon.

## TOBIKO
Flying fish roe, usually dyed bright orange, frequently used in the preparation of California rolls.
*(See "On the menu," page 66.)*

## TOFU
Bean curd, extremely high in protein and easily digestible. Japanese tofu, which is softer, whiter, and more delicately flavoured than the Chinese type, melts in the mouth.

## TORO
Part of the Tuna's belly. It is considered a great delicacy. *(See "On the menu," page 67.)*

## TSUKIDASHI
Side dishes or surprise accompaniments to a sushi meal. For instance, the chef may present you with a fresh cucumber sliced in a spiral or spread like a fan, or a cold, briny gobou, a slender, carrot-like root we know as burdock in English.

## TUNA
*(See MAGURO)*

## UKI USU ZUKURI
*(See SUZUKI)*

## UMEBOSHI
Salted marinated plums, a delicacy often served with plain cooked white rice.

# ■THE ESSENTIALS

## UNAGI
Freshwater eel. Unagi is similar to anago (marine eel) in colour and taste. Instead of being boiled first, however, it is grilled, then glazed with a mixture of soy sauce, sugar and eel broth. The sauce makes it taste sweet and rich. It should be eaten without any dipping sauce.
(See "On the menu," page 70.)

## UNI
The gonads of the sea urchin. Brave sushi eaters in many parts of the world consider uni a great delicacy. Soft in texture and served held in place with a band of nori, it has a delicious, subtle, nutlike flavour.
(See "On the menu," page 71.)

## URAMAKI
"Inside-out" *sushi*, made with the rice outside and the *nori* inside.

## VINEGAR for sushi
(See KOMEZU)

## WAKAME
A type of seaweed that comes in dried form. Once reconstituted, it turns bright green. Wakame is used in miso soups as well as salads.

## WASABI
Green Japanese horseradish mustard, a pungent aromatic spice derived from the root of the wasabi plant, grown only in Japan. It has antibacterial properties and is rich in Vitamin C. The olive-green roots are grown in shallow water. Because fresh wasabi is very expensive and hard to find outside Japan, cheaper powder and paste alternatives are often used.

## YELLOWTAIL TUNA
(*See HAMACHI*)

## YONEZU
Rice vinegar used to prepare sushi. The traditional method of brewing rice vinegar uses organically grown rice and spring water. The brewed vinegar is mixed with sugar and salt and used to prepare rice for sushi-making.

## YUKIWA-MAKI
Another name for inside-out *sushi*.

# ■ MY FAVOURITE SUSHI BARS AND RESTAURANTS

Name : _____
Address : _____
Phone : _____

_____
_____
_____
_____

Name : _____
Address : _____
Phone : _____

_____
_____
_____
_____

Name : _____
Address : _____
Phone : _____

_____
_____
_____
_____

Name : _____
Address : _____
Phone : _____

_____
_____
_____
_____

Name : _____
Address : _____
Phone : _____

_____
_____
_____

Name : _____
Address : _____
Phone : _____
_____
_____
_____

Name : _____
Address : _____
Phone : _____
_____
_____
_____

Name : _____
Address : _____
Phone : _____
_____
_____
_____

Name : _____
Address : _____
Phone : _____
_____
_____
_____

Name : _____
Address : _____
Phone : _____
_____
_____
_____

# ■ INDEX "ON THE MENU"

AJI MACKEREL p.18

ALASKA ALASKA p.19

AMA-EBI SWEET SHRIMP p.20

ANAGO SEA EEL p.21

AVOCADO AVOCADO p.22

BENI JAKE PACIFIC SALMON p.23

CALIFORNIA ROLL CALIFORNIA ROLL p.24

CHIRASHIZUSHI CHIRASHIZUSHI p.25

EBI SHRIMP p.26

FUGU BLOWFISH p.27

FUTOMAKI FUTOMAKI p.28

HAMACHI YELLOW TAIL TUNA p.29

HIRAME FLOUNDER p.30

HOKKIGAI SURF CLAM p.31

HOTATEGAI SCALLOP p.32

IKA SQUID p.33

IKURA SALMON ROE p.34

INARIZUSHI TOFU POCKET p.35

IWASHI SARDINE p.36

KAMIKAZE KAMIKAZE p.37

KAMPYO FLOWER ROOTS p.38

KANI SNOW CRAB p.39

KANI-KAMA CRAB STICK p.40

KAPPA MAKI CUCUMBER ROLL p.41

KAZUNOKO HERRING ROE p.42

KUNSEI SYAKE SMOKED SALMON p.43

KOHADA GRIZZARD SHAD p.44

MAGURO RED TUNA p.45

MASAGO SMELT ROE p.46

MIRUGAI KING CLAM p.47

NEGI HAMACHI YELLOW TAIL TUNA p.48

NEGI HAMACHI TEMAKI
YELLOW TAIL TUNA p.49

OSHINKO MAKI OSHINKO MAKI p.50

PHILADELPHIA PHILADELPHIA p.51

RISING SUN SCALLOP AND TOBIKO p.52

SABA OILY MACKEREL p.53

SALMON SKIN GRILLED SALMON SKIN p.54

SHIRO MAGURO ALBACORE p.55

SPICY TUNA MAKI SPICY TUNA p.56

SPICY TUNA GOUNKAN SPICY TUNA p.57

SPIDER ROLL SPIDER ROLL p.58

SUZUKI SEA BASS p.59

SYAKE ATLANTIC SALMON p.60

SYAKE MAKI SALMON p.61

TAI RED SNAPPER p.62

TAKO OCTOPUS TAKO p.63

TAMAGO EGG CLUSTER p.64

TEKKA MAKI TUNA ROLLS p.65

TOBIKO FLYING FISH ROE p.66

TORO FATTY TUNA p.67

UME-KYU UME-KYU p.68

UNA-KYU GRILLED EEL p.69

UNAGI FRESH WATER EEL p.70

UNI SEA URCHIN ROE p.71

*Send your comments to*
masteringsushi@leporemedia.com